ABCs
of
Who *I* Am *in* Christ!

ABCs of Who I Am in Christ!
I Am what God says I Am!
Created by Kathleen Schubitz

Copyright © 2012-2013 by Kathleen Schubitz.

Published by:
RPJ & COMPANY, INC.
Web Site: www.rpjandco1417.com | www.rpjandco.com
Orlando, Florida, U.S.A.

Scripture references from the King James Version of the Bible. All rights reserved.

ISBN-13: 978-1-937770-30-3

Cover image: Sarininka @ fotolia.com
Cover design by Kathleen Schubitz

Interior Design Consultant: Cat Sanders

Printed in the United States of America

For every believer
who desires simple reminders
of who we are
and what we have
been called to be
in the Kingdom of God!

Table of Contents

Published by:

RPJ & COMPANY, INC.
www.rpjandco.com

ABCs
of
Who I Am in Christ!

I am what
God says
I am!

Created by Kathleen Schubitz

Acknowledgments

To all my leaders, past and present, who chose to bring revelation forth, regardless of setting, and the Spirit of the Living God to make the simple truths active and alive in me.

I am grateful for Linda Markowitz and her ministry. Her keen spirit to train and equip the saints of God makes a tremendous impact in the lives of the searching and hungry souls. She is my most recent teacher and motivator of God's Word, and some of her inspiring *I Am* statements have been included in this book.

Wandra Melnick, for her steadfastness and determination to help whenever I called. For all her contributions, research and dedication.

To the Spirit of the living God, thank you for stirring me to walk in a greater knowledge of truth and understanding of the written word.

More books by KATHLEEN SCHUBITZ

...In His Presence:
Intimate moments with your Savior
(B/W and Color versions)

ABC Journal to Freedom
I Am What God Says I Am!

ABC Woman Finds Freedom

ABCs of Who I Am in Christ!
(for women)

Finding Purpose after Abuse
Inspiration for all those seeking freedom from their past

His Heart Calls: Love notes from God's Word
(366 Day Devotional - KJV & Contemporary versions)

Journal to Freedom

Personal Poetic Promises from God's Word

Scripture Keys
Inspiring words for your journey

Weekly Planner/Devotional
52-Week planner for any year with poetic devotions

FIND OUR BOOKS AT MOST ONLINE STORES AND
WWW.RPJANDCO1417.COM

Author's Note

ABCs of Who I Am in Christ! arose from a simple message given to me years ago. It has been compiled throughout my Christian walk and reflects personal beliefs and maturity through years of a Spirit-filled life.

Many statements shared here did not originate with me, but are familiar to many as they have been taught in Christian circles for years. Together in a pocket-sized companion they simply bring more firm knowledge and remembrance of who we are according to the Word of God. Such a collection is never complete...words and statements will grow as the Lord inspires each reader with new thoughts and ideas.

Space is provided throughout this book for writing your own statements. Allow God's Words to become active and alive for yourself and others. Be all you have been called to be according to His Word, and enjoy your discovery of who *you* are in Christ!

- Kathy

I am Abiding in the shadow of the Almighty!
PSALM 91:1

I am Able to comfort others who are in trouble
by the comfort I have received of God!
2 CORINTHIANS 1:4

I am Able to do all things through Christ
Who strengthens me!
PHILIPPIANS 4:13

I am Able to escape temptation because
He makes a way!
1 CORINTHIANS 10:13

I am Abounding in love toward others!
1 THESSALONIANS 3:12

I am Abounding in faith and knowledge!
2 CORINTHIANS 8:7

I am Abundantly blessed!
GENESIS 9:7

I am Accepted in Christ!
2 CORINTHIANS 5:9, EPHESIANS 1:6

I am Accepting the treasures of darkness and
hidden riches of secret places!
ISAIAH 45:3

I am Accepting God's spoken word to me!
2 SAMUEL 7:25

I am Accomplishing God's spoken word!
ISAIAH 55:11

I am Achieving my potential in Christ!
ROMANS 6:4

I am Acknowledging godly wisdom to gain
knowledge and understanding!
PROVERBS 2:6

I am Acknowledging the Lord and He
directs my path!
PROVERBS 3:6

I am Adjusting my thoughts to line up with
God's Word!
ACTS 17:11

I am Adopted into the family of God!
ROMANS 8:15

I am Adopted as His child!
EPHESIANS 1:5

I am Adorned by the King of Kings!
REVELATION 21:2

I am Advancing in the things for which I have
been called!
ESTHER 5:11, 10:2

I am Affectionate toward others with
brotherly love!
ROMANS 12:10

I am Agreeing with God's plan for my life!
REVELATION 17:17

I am Agreeing with God's spoken word to me!
JOB 23:12, EZEKIEL 33:30

I am Aligned with the Word of God!
HEBREWS 4:12, 1 CORINTHIANS 1:10

I am Alive by the Holy Spirit living in me!
2 SAMUEL 23:2

I am Alive together with Christ!
EPHESIANS 2:5

I am Allowing the Spirit of God to rule and
reign in my life!
PSALM 31:5

I am an Ambassador for Christ!
PROVERBS 13:17, ISAIAH 33:7

I am an Advocate for Christ!
1 JOHN 2:1

I am an Atmosphere changer!
ROMANS 12:2

I am Anchored in Christ Jesus!
HEBREWS 6:19

I am Anointed by God!
1 JOHN 2:27, LUKE 4:18

I am Anointed with God's Spirit!
ISAIAH 61:1

I am Anointed with oil; my cup runneth over!
PSALM 23:5

I am Anointed with the oil of gladness!
PSALM 45:7

I am Appealing to the God of Heaven!
NEHEMIAH 2:4

I am Appearing with Him in glory!
COLOSSIANS 3:4

I am Appointed by God!
1 CHRONICLES 9:29, 15:19, LUKE 22:29

I am Appreciative of what God has
done for me!
JOHN 1:14

I am Apprehending a greater measure of
God's truth!
PSALM 25:5

I am Asking for godly wisdom!
MATTHEW 7:7, 2 CHRONICLES 1:11

I am Assured that all things work together
for good!
ROMANS 8:28

I am Attentive to godliness!
NEHEMIAH 1:6, PROVERBS 5:1

I am Authentic!
1 PETER 2:12

I am Avenged by the Lord!
ROMANS 12:19

I am Awakening to my true calling in
Christ Jesus!
1 CORINTHIANS 7:20, EPHESIANS 4:4

I am the Apple of His eye!
PSALM 17:8

I am walking Above and not beneath!
DEUTERONOMY 28:13

I am a Beloved child of God!
SONG OF SOLOMON 7:10

I am a Burden bearer!
2 CHRONICLES 34:13

I am Baptized by the Holy Spirit!
1 CORINTHIANS 12:13

I am Bearing witness to Jesus!
JOHN 5:32, 8:18

I am Beautifully created for His glory!
PSALM 48:2, ECCLESIASTES 3:11

I am Becoming new in Christ!
2 CORINTHIANS 5:17

I am Becoming who God made me to be!
1 CORINTHIANS 1:17

I am Beholding His glory!
ISAIAH 60:2

I am Being changed from glory to glory!
2 CORINTHIANS 3:18

I am Believing all things are possible for me!
LUKE 1:37

I am Believing all things work together
for my good!
ROMANS 8:28

I am Believing on Him that I will not abide
in darkness!
JOHN 12:46

I am Believing on the Son Who has given
me everlasting life!
JOHN 3:36

I am Bestowed with blessings!
EXODUS 32:29

I am Bestowed with God's grace!
1 CORINTHIANS 15:10, 1 JOHN 3:1

I am Betrothed to my Maker!
HOSEA 2:19, 2:20

I am Binding my soul to the will of God!
ROMANS 12:2, NUMBERS 30:2

I am Birthing that which God has
planted in me!
GALATIANS 4:19

I am Blameless in Christ!
EPHESIANS 1:4, 1 THESSALONIANS 3:13, 5:23

I am Blessed and renewed in knowledge!
COLOSSIANS 3:10

I am Blessed because my transgressions
are forgiven!
ISAIAH 43:25

I am Blessed beyond measure!
PROVERBS 3:10, 10:22, LUKE 6:38

I am Blessed in the city and blessed in the field!
DEUTERONOMY 28:3

I am Blessed in the God of truth and shall be
blessed in the earth!
PSALM 115:15

I am Blessed of the Lord which made heaven
and earth!
PSALM 115:15

I am Blessed to be hungry and blessed
when I weep!
LUKE 6:21

I am Blessed to give!
ACTS 20:35

I am Blessed with an ear to hear my
Father's voice!
REVELATION 2:7, 2:29

I am Blessed with daily benefits!
PSALM 68:19

I am Blessed with every spiritual blessing!
EPHESIANS 1:3

I am Blessed with eyes to see!
MATTHEW 7:5

I am Blessed with peace!
PSALM 29:11

I am Blessing myself and others with words
pleasing to the Lord!
DEUTERONOMY 30:19

I am Blood-washed!
EPHESIANS 1:7

I am Bold as a lion!
PROVERBS 28:1

I am Boldly coming to the throne of grace!
HEBREWS 4:16

I am Born into the Kingdom for such a
time as this!
ECCLESIASTES 3:2

I am Born of God and the evil one cannot
touch me!
1 JOHN 5:18

I am Breaking enemy assignments over
my loved ones!
2, PETER 3:9, ISAIAH 28:17-19

I am Breaking every assignment I've ever made
with the enemy!
ISAIAH 28:17-19

I am Breaking through to my glorious future!
JEREMIAH 29:11

I am Bringing into captivity every thought
to the obedience of Christ!
2 CORINTHIANS 10:5

I am Building my faith in God!
MATTHEW 17:20

I am Building my house with wisdom!
PROVERBS 9:1

I am Building relationships and trust in God!
PROVERBS 3:5

I am His Beloved and His banner over
me is love!
SONG OF SOLOMON 2:4

I am in a Blood covenant relationship
with the Lord!
GENESIS 17:7, HEBREWS 13:20

I am my Beloved's, and his desire is toward me!
SONG OF SOLOMON 7:10

I am the Breath of the Almighty!
JOB 33:4

I am the Bride of Christ!
ISAIAH 61:10

I am a Cheerful giver!
2 CORINTHIANS 9:7

I am a Child loved by God!
GALATIANS 2:20

I am a Child of the King!
PROVERBS 22:1, GALATIANS 3:26

I am a Chosen vessel!
JOHN 15:16, ACTS 9:15

I am a Citizen of Heaven!
PHILIPPIANS 3:20

I am a Conqueror through Him who loves me!
ROMANS 8:37

I am a Courageous child of God!
PSALM 16:9

I am Calling upon Him!
ISAIAH 55:6

**I am Calling upon the Lord in the day of
my trouble because He will answer me!**
PSALM 86:7

I am Calmed by the Peacemaker!
PSALM 107:29

I am Careful for nothing, but by prayer and
supplication with thanksgiving, letting my
requests be known unto God!
PHILIPPIANS 4:6

I am Casting all my care upon Him!
1 PETER 5:7

I am Ceasing from anger and will forsake wrath!
PSALM 37:8

I am Celebrated by the King!
ISAIAH 62:2, 38:18

I am Changed from glory to glory!
2 CORINTHIANS 3:18

I am Character-building through my experiences!
ROMANS 5:4

I am Choosing to be thankful in all things!
1 THESSALONIANS 5:18

I am Choosing to let every prisoner go free!
MATTHEW 5:44

I am Choosing to live in God's truth!
JOHN 8:32

I am Chosen and dearly loved!
COLOSSIANS 3:12, 1 THESSALONIANS 1:4

I am Christ-minded!
1 CORINTHIANS 2:16

I am Clay in the Potter's hands!
JEREMIAH 18:6, ISAIAH 64:8

I am Cleansed from all sin!
2 CORINTHIANS 7:1, 1 JOHN 1:7

I am Clothed in humility!
PROVERBS 22:4

I am Comforted by God's Word!
PSALM 23:4, 94:19, ISAIAH 49:13

I am Commissioned to preach the gospel!
MARK 16:15

I am Committing my works unto the Lord and my thoughts shall be established!
PROVERBS 15:22, 16:3, PSALM 37:5

I am Committed to the Holy One!
2 TIMOTHY 1:12

I am Communing with the Lord!
LUKE 24:15, PSALM 77:6

I am Compassed about with wings of deliverance!
PSALM 32:7

I am Compassionate toward others!
1 PETER 3:8

I am Complete in Christ!
COLOSSIANS 2:10

I am Complete with God's love!
COLOSSIANS 4:12, 2:10

I am Confessing aloud what God says about me!
ROMANS 10:9-10

I am Confident in the God of my salvation!
1 SAMUEL 2:1

I am Confident that God will perfect the work
He has begun in me!
PHILIPPIANS 1:6

I am Consecrated unto the Lord!
1 KINGS 13:33, EXODUS 32:29

I am Consecrating every relationship unto God!
RUTH 1:14

I am Considerate of others!
HEBREWS 10:24

I am Content in the things of God!
PHILIPPIANS 4:11, 1 TIMOTHY 6:6

I am Continually surrendering to the Holy Spirit!
LUKE 4:1

I am Counseled by the Lord!
EXODUS 18:19, PSALM 16:7

I am Covered all the day long!
ISAIAH 51:16

I am Covered with his feathers, and under
his wings I will trust!
PSALM 91:4

I am Created in God's own image!
GENESIS 1:27

I am Creating special memories with my Savior!
LUKE 1:47

I am Crossing over to my promised land!
DEUTERONOMY 19:8

I am Crowned with glory and honor!
PSALM 8:5

I am Crowned with lovingkindness and
tender mercies!
PSALM 103:4, 21:3

I am Crucified with Christ!
GALATIANS 2:20

I am in Covenant relationship with God!
DEUTERONOMY 7:9, PSALM 89:3

I am a Delegate for Christ!
1 CHRONICLES 16:4, MATTHEW 27:10

I am a Devoted child of God!
PSALM 119:38

I am a Doer of the Word!
JAMES 1:22

I am a Dwelling for the Holy Spirit!
EPHESIANS 2:22

I am Dancing with Jesus!
PSALM 30:11, SONG OF SOLOMON 2:6

I am Declaring His glory and marvelous works among the nations!
1 CHRONICLES 16:24

I am Declaring my freedom in Christ!
LUKE 4:18

I am Decreeing God's Word over my life!
JOB 22:28

I am Dedicated to Almighty God!
EXODUS 32:29

I am Deepening my relationship with the Lord!
PSALM 42:7

I am Deliberately following Christ!
1 PETER 2:21

I am Delightfully trusting in the Lord!
PROVERBS 3:5, PSALM 119:174

I am Delighting myself in the Lord!
PSALM 37:4

I am Delivered by the Hand of God!
PSALM 116:8, 22:8, PROVERBS 11:8

I am Delivered from evil and the violent man!
PSALM 18:48, 2 TIMOTHY 4:18

I am Denouncing enemy lies!
MATTHEW 16:23

I am Depositing into my heavenly bank account!
MALACHI 3:10, HEBREWS 6:10

I am Desiring God's best for my life!
JEREMIAH 29:11

I am Desperate for a move of God!
PSALM 68:8, 2 PETER 1:21

I am Destiny-driven!
ROMANS 8:4

I am Determined to be single-minded!
JAMES 1:8

I am Determined to follow Jesus!
1 PETER 2:21

I am Devoted unto the Lord!
LEVITICUS 27:28B

I am Dignified!
PSALM 40:4, 119:15

I am Diligent in my walk with Christ!
2 TIMOTHY 2:15

I am Diligently seeking the Lord!
HEBREWS 11:6

I am Directing my prayer unto the Lord!
PSALM 5:3

I am Discarding my old identity!
ROMANS 6:6

I am Discerning God's will for my life!
GALATIANS 1:4

I am Disciplined by the Lord!
JOB 36:9-11

I am Discovering my identity in Christ!
COLOSSIANS 3:10

I am Disengaging from ungodliness!
TITUS 2:12

I am Divinely inspired by the living Word!
2 TIMOTHY 3:16

I am Divinely walking in health!
PROVERBS 16:24

I am Drawing from the Living Well!
PROVERBS 5:15

I am Drawing nigh to God so He will draw nigh unto me!
JAMES 4:8

I am Drawing water from the well of salvation!
ISAIAH 12:3

I am Dwelling in His Everlasting Arms!
DEUTERONOMY 33:27

I am Dwelling in His presence!
PSALM 16:11

I am Dwelling in His secret place!
PSALM 91:1

I am Dwelling in perfect peace!
ISAIAH 26:3

I am Dwelling in safety!
EZEKIEL 34:28, PSALM 4:8

I am Dwelling in the house of the Lord for ever!
PSALM 23:6, 27:4

I am Dwelling in the shelter of the Most High!
PSALM 91:1

I am an Eternal being through Christ!
ROMANS 6:23

I am an Expression of the life of Christ!
COLOSSIANS 3:4

I am Embraced by His right hand!
SONG OF SOLOMON 2:6

I am Emerging as a new creation!
JOB 23:10

I am Emotionally stable and secure in
God's Word!
JUDGES 18:10, JOB 11:18

I am Empowered by faith!
ROMANS 4:20

I am Emulating the character of Jesus!
2 CORINTHIANS 13:11

I am Encompassed with a shield!
PSALM 5:12, 17:9

I am Encouraged by the Word of God!
EPHESIANS 4:29

I am Endearing toward the Lord!
COLOSSIANS 3:2

I am Endued with grace!
JAMES 3:13

I am Endued with power from on high!
LUKE 24:49

I am Enduring patiently!
REVELATION 2:3, HEBREWS 12:2

I am Enduring until the end!
MATTHEW 10:22

I am Energetic in the things of the Lord!
ISAIAH 40:31

**I am Energizing every cell of my body with
the Word!**
ROMANS 8:12-14

I am Enlightened to know the hope of His calling!
EPHESIANS 1:18

I am Enlisted in the Lord's battle!
ISAIAH 54:17

I am Enriched in His presence!
1 CORINTHIANS 1:5

**I am Entering His gates with thanksgiving and
into His courts with praise!**
PSALM 100:4

I am Entering the promised land!
DEUTERONOMY 6:3

I am Enveloped by my Savior!
PSALM 34:7

I am Entrusting the Lord with my life!
2 SAMUEL 22:3

I am Equipped with God's Word!
MARK 6:8

I am Espoused to the Holy One!
2 CORINTHIANS 11:2

I am Established by the Lord and
kept from evil!
2 THESSALONIANS 3:3

I am Established with an everlasting covenant!
EZEKIEL 16:60

I am Esteemed by the Lord!
PROVERBS 17:28

I am Eternally blessed!
JOHN 3:15

I am Exalted by the God of my salvation!
PSALM 18:46, EXODUS 15:2

I am Exalting others in Christ!
MATTHEW 23:12

I am Examined by the Redeemer!
LUKE 23:14

I am Examining my heart before
condemning others!
PSALM 26:2, 2 CORINTHIANS 13:5

I am Exceedingly blessed!
GENESIS 17:2

I am Exchanging enemy lies for God's truth!
JOHN 16:13

I am Exemplifying Christ in my daily living!
JOHN 13:15

I am Exercising godly authority!
MATTHEW 20:25, 1 TIMOTHY 4:7

I am Exhaling the living Word of God!
EXODUS 28:3, ROMANS 15:6

I am Exhorting others in the Lord!
1 THESSALONIANS 4:1, 5:14

I am Expanding in godly wisdom!
EXODUS 31:3

I am Expediently growing in the Lord!
JOHN 16:7, 11:50

I am Expounding the Word!
HABAKKUK 2:2

I am Expressing the love of God!
EPHESIANS 4:15

I am Expunging enemy lies from my mind!
2 CORINTHIANS 10:5

I am Exuberant in Christ!
PSALM 106:8

I am Exuding Joy!
JUDE 1:24, PSALM 63:5

I am the Essence of God's creation!
2 PETER 1:4

I am a Faithful child of God!
MATTHEW 25:21, EPHESIANS 1:1

I am a Follower of God and walk in love!
EPHESIANS 5:1

I am a Follower of Jesus Christ!
ROMANS 14:19

I am a Forerunner with the Lord!
HEBREWS 6:20

I am a Friend of Jesus!
JOHN 15:15, JAMES 2:23

I am Faithful and true!
PSALM 33:4

I am Favored by God and man!
1 SAMUEL 2:26

I am Fearfully and wonderfully made!
PSALM 139:14

I am Feeding on spiritual food for strength!
PSALM 28:9, JEREMIAH 3:15

I am Fervent in spirit!
JAMES 5:16, ACTS 18:25

I am Filled with all joy and peace in believing!
ROMANS 15:13

I am Filled with everlasting Joy!
ISAIAH 51:11

I am Filled with gentleness!
2 SAMUEL 22:36, 2 CORINTHIANS 10:1, GALATIANS 5:22

I am Filled with glory and strength because
He lives in me!
PHILIPPIANS 1:11, HABAKKUK 3:19

I am Filled with God's faithfulness!
PSALM 89:1

I am Filled with the fruit of righteousness!
PHILIPPIANS 1:11

I am Filled with the Word of God!
ACTS 4:31

I am Financially free!
MALACHI 3:10

I am Finding grace in the sight of the Lord!
GENESIS 19:19

I am Finding grace to help in time of need!
HEBREWS 4:16

I am Finding rest in Jesus!
MATTHEW 11:28-30

I am Finishing the course set before me!
ACTS 13:25, 20:24, 2 CORINTHIANS 8:11

I am Fit for the kingdom of God!
LUKE 9:62

I am Fixing my heart and eyes upon Jesus!
PSALM 5:3, ISAIAH 45:22

I am Flooded with God's presence!
JOHN 7:38

I am Flourishing as a branch of the Vine!
PSALM 92:14, PROVERBS 11:28

I am Focused on God's provision for my life!
GENESIS 42:25, CHRONICLES 29:19

I am Focused on the Christ nature of my being!
PSALM 25:15, 141:8

I am Focused on the things of God!
MATTHEW 6:33

I am Followed by goodness and mercy
all the days of my life!
PSALM 23:6

I am Following after things which make
for peace!
ROMANS 14:19

I am Following godly counsel!
PSALM 73:24

I am Following Him and will be made a
fisher of men!
MATTHEW 4:19

I am Following the light and shall not walk
in darkness!
JOHN 8:12

I am Forgiven of every iniquity!
PSALM 32:1, 103:3

I am Forgiving of others!
EPHESIANS 4:32

I am Forgiving others as the Lord forgives me!
MATTHEW 6:14

I am Found in Him!
DEUTERONOMY 4:29, PSALM 32:6

I am Free of anxiety!
1 PETER 5:7

I am Free from the sins of my past!
ROMANS 8:1-2, 2 TIMOTHY 2:22

I am Free of every sickness and infirmity!
HEBREWS 4:15

I am Fruitful!
MATTHEW 12:33

I am Fulfilled in God's plan for my life!
ROMANS 13:8

I am Fulfilling my spiritual destiny!
ROMANS 8:4

I am Full of goodness and filled with
all knowledge!
ROMANS 15:14

I am Full of joy!
1 JOHN 1:4

I am highly Favored!
PROVERBS 12:2

I am in Fellowship with the Lord and walk
in the light!
1 JOHN 1:6-7

I am a Gate-keeper!
EPHESIANS 6:18, 2 CHRONICLES 34:13

I am a Gatherer!
RUTH 2:7, 1 CHRONICLES 16:35

I am a God pleaser!
COLOSSIANS 1:10, 1 THESSALONIANS 2:4

I am a Good listener!
MATTHEW 11:15

I am a Graceful child of God!
GENESIS 39:4

I am a vessel of God's grace!
RUTH 2:10

I am a vessel of Goodness!
PSALM 21:3, 107:9

I am a vessel of His Gentleness!
2 SAMUEL 22:36

I am filled with Holy Ghost power!
ACTS 2:4, EPHESIANS 5:18

I am Gaining territory for God's kingdom!
EXODUS 29:46

I am Girded with gladness!
PSALM 30:11

I am Girded with God's strength!
PSALM 18:32, 18:39

I am Given to know the mysteries of the kingdom of God!
LUKE 8:10

I am Giving God praise in all things!
PSALM 139:14

I am Glad for the Lord has done great things for me!
PSALM 126:2

I am Glorifying my Father which is in heaven when I let my light shine before men!
MATTHEW 5:16

I am God's workmanship!
EPHESIANS 2:10

I am Good seed planted in the field!
MATTHEW 13:38

I am Gracious in the Lord!
PSALM 116:5

I am Grateful for all things!
DEUTERONOMY 4:7

I am Grounded in the Word of God!
COLOSSIANS 1:23

I am Growing in grace and knowledge!
2 PETER 3:18

I am Guided by His counsel!
PSALM 73:24

I am Guided by the Holy Spirit living inside of me!
PSALM 32:8

I am Guided by the skillfulness of His hands!
PSALM 78:72

I am Guided continually and my soul
is satisfied!
ISAIAH 58:11

I am Guided into all truth!
JOHN 16:13

I am Guided into the ways of peace!
PSALM 31:3

I am Guided with His eye!
PSALM 32:8

I am of Good cheer because He has
overcome the world!
JOHN 16:33

I am a Hurdle overcomer!
JOHN 16:33, 1 JOHN 4:4, REVELATION 21:7

I am a vessel of God's Holiness!
PSALM 96:9

I am a vessel of Honor!
2 TIMOTHY 2:21

**I am an Heir according to the
hope of eternal life!**
TITUS 3:7

I am an Heir of God and a joint heir with Jesus!
PSALM 94:14

I am clothed with Honor!
PSALM 104:1

I am Happy because He made me free!
ROMANS 8:2

**I am Happy to find godly wisdom and
get understanding!**
PROVERBS 3:13

I am Healed of every disease!
PSALM 103:2-3, PROVERBS 4:22, 16:24

I am Healed with His stripes!
ISAIAH 53:5

I am Hearing the Spirit of God!
MATTHEW 11:15, 13:43, MARK 4:9, JOHN 8:47

I am Hearing His lovingkindness every morning!
PSALM 143:8

I am Heaven-bound!
MATTHEW 16:19

I am Heavenly-minded!
EPHESIANS 1:3

I am Held up by His right hand!
PSALM 145:14

I am Helped in times of trouble!
PSALM 46:1

I am Helped and my heart greatly rejoices!
PSALM 5:11

I am Hid under the shadow of His wings!
PSALM 17:8

I am Hid with Christ!
COLOSSIANS 3:3, PSALM 32:7

I am Highly favored!
1 SAMUEL 2:26, PSALM 5:12

I am Holy because He is holy!
LEVITICUS 21:6

I am Holy in all manner of conversation!
1 PETER 1:15

I am Honored because I fear the Lord!
PSALM 15:4

I am Honored by the One who made me!
PSALM 91:15

I am Honoring my father and my mother!
EXODUS 20:12

I am Honoring the Lord with my substance and
the firstfruits of all my increase!
PROVERBS 3:9

I am Hopeful in God!
ROMANS 8:24

I am Humble, gentle, patient and lovingly
tolerant of others!
EPHESIANS 4:2

I am Humbled under His mighty hand, that I
may be exalted in due time!
1 PETER 5:6

I am in Harmony with Creation!
GENESIS 1:28

I am the Head and not the tail!
DEUTERONOMY 28:13

I am a vessel of Integrity!
1 KINGS 9:4, PSALM 7:8, 26:11, PROVERBS 20:7

I am an Imitator of Jesus Christ!
1 CORINTHIANS 7:22, 1 JOHN 3:2

I am an Inspiring child of God!
JOB 32:8

I am an Instrument of righteousness!
ROMANS 6:13

I am an Intercessor for God's people!
HEBREWS 7:25

I am Illuminated through prayer and obedience!
MATTHEW 13:43

I am Immovable when I stand upon the Rock!
PSALM 89:26, 1 CORINTHIANS 15:58, 10:4

I am Impressing others to live in truth!
ISAIAH 43:9, JEREMIAH 33:6

I am Improving through maturity!
ROMANS 8:27

I am Inclining myself in God's presence!
GENESIS 24:26, 1 CHRONICLES 29:20, PSALM 95:6

I am Included in God's family!
Ephesians 1:13

I am Indeed blessed of the Lord!
1 Chronicles 4:10

I am Indigenous in the things of the Lord!
2 Peter 3:18

I am Influencing others in godly ways!
Psalm 79:13

I am Influential in God's kingdom!
Daniel 2:37

I am Infused with kingdom power!
1 Corinthians 4:20

I am Infused with the spirit of God!
Acts 2:4

I am Inheriting substance and He fills
my treasures!
Proverbs 8:21

I am Inseparable from the love of God!
Romans 8:35, 8:39

I am Insightful in godly matters!
Isaiah 11:3, Hebrews 4:12

I am Inspired by the living Word of God!
Job 32:8

I am Instant in season and out of season!
2 TIMOTHY 4:2

I am Instructed and taught in the way
which I shall go!
PSALM 32:8

I am Intelligent!
ROMANS 7:25

I am Intentionally working for the
Kingdom of God!
ROMANS 8:28

I am Invoking the Holy Spirit continually!
JEREMIAH 33:3

I am the Image of God!
GENESIS 1:27

I am a Jewel in the King's crown!
MALACHI 3:17, PHILIPPIANS 4:1

I am a Joint heir with Christ!
ROMANS 8:17

I am filled with Joy and led with peace!
ISAIAH 55:12

I am Joined unto the Lord in one spirit!
1 CORINTHIANS 6:17

I am Joyful in the Lord!
PSALM 35:9

I am Joyful through my trials!
JAMES 1:2

I am Joyfully received by my Father!
LUKE 19:6

I am Judged by my righteousness and integrity!
PSALM 7:8, 25:21

I am Judging no man!
MATTHEW 7:1, 7:2

I am Justified by faith and have peace with God!
ROMANS 5:1

I am Justified freely by His grace!
TITUS 3:7, ROMANS 3:24, 5:1

I am Justified by my words!
MATTHEW 12:37

I am on a Journey with the Lord!
1 THESSALONIANS 5:17, PSALM 62:5

I am a Key to the Kingdom!
ISAIAH 22:22, REVELATION 3:7

I am a Kindred spirit in the Kingdom of God!
PSALM 96:7

I am a King and priest of my home!
1 PETER 2:9

I am a vessel of Kindness!
1 SAMUEL 20:14, 2 SAMUEL 2:6

I am Keeping His Word in my heart!
1 KINGS 9:4

I am Keeping time for the Lord in every day!
ZEPHANIAH 3:20

I am Kept and preserved!
PSALM 12:7

I am Kept in perfect peace because my mind is stayed on the Lord!
ISAIAH 26:3

I am Kind-hearted!
1 KINGS 3:6

I am Kingdom-minded!
2 CORINTHIANS 13:11

I am Kissed in the Lord's Presence!
2 CORINTHIANS 13:12

I am Kneeling before the Lord!
PSALM 95:6

I am Knit together with Christ!
COLOSSIANS 2:2

I am Knocking until my answer comes!
MATTHEW 7:7

I am Knowledgeable of the truth, therefore
the truth makes me free!
JOHN 8:32

I am Known by my heart and my thoughts!
PSALM 139:23

I am Known by the fruit in my life!
MATTHEW 7:20

I am a Leader for the Lord!
ISAIAH 55:4

I am a Lender, not a borrower!
DEUTERONOMY 28:12

I am a Life-changer!
JOHN 10:10

I am a Light in the world!
MATTHEW 5:14

I am a Living Stone in God's Kingdom!
1 PETER 2:5

I am a vessel of Love!
ROMANS 9:23

I am Laying up treasures in heaven!
LUKE 12:34

I am Learning to forgive myself!
PSALM 25:18

I am Led by the Spirit of God!
ROMANS 8:14

I am Led in His truth for He is the God of
my salvation!
PSALM 25:5

I am Led in the path of righteousness for
His name's sake!
PSALM 23:3

I am Led into the land of uprightness!
PSALM 143:10

I am Liberated from the law of sin and death!
ROMANS 8:2

I am Lifting up my hands to the God of heaven!
GENESIS 14:22

I am Lifted up from the gates of death!
PSALM 9:13

I am Like a watered garden and a spring
of water, whose waters fail not!
ISAIAH 58:11

I am Listening for my Father's instructions!
PROVERBS 4:4-6, 4:20

I am Lively because He paid a great price!
JOHN 3:16

I am Living and walking in the Spirit!
GALATIANS 5:25

I am Living by faith in the Son of God!
GALATIANS 2:20

I am Living for the King!
JEREMIAH 38:17

I am Living in God's promise of love!
JAMES 1:12

I am Living in prosperity as I keep the
Lord's statutes!
1 SAMUEL 25:6, 1 KINGS 2:3

I am Living in the land of plenty!
DEUTERONOMY 28:11, PHILIPPIANS 4:19

I am Living in the spirit of power, and love,
and a sound mind!
2 TIMOTHY 1:7

I am Living in unity with God's people!
PSALM 133:1

I am Living my life pleasing to the Lord!
PSALM 19:14, COLOSSIANS 1:10, 1 JOHN 3:22

I am Longsuffering!
1 TIMOTHY 1:16

I am Looking to the Author and Finisher
of my faith!
HEBREWS 12:2

I am Losing my life for the sake of Christ!
MATTHEW 10:39

I am Loved because He first loved me!
1 JOHN 4:19, DEUTERONOMY 7:8, 23:5

I am Loved by God!
JOHN 3:16

I am Lovely!
PHILIPPIANS 4:8

**I am Loving the Lord with all my heart,
soul and strength!**
MARK 12:33

I am Loving toward others!
PSALM 26:3

I am a Messenger for the Lord!
MALACHI 2:7

I am a Minister of the Gospel!
ROMANS 15:16

I am filled with Mercy!
LUKE 1:50, ROMANS 9:23

I am Made by the spirit of God!
JOB 33:4

I am Made free by God's Son!
JOHN 8:36

I am Made free from sin!
ROMANS 6:22

I am Made in His likeness!
PSALM 1:15, 17:15

I am Made perfectly in love!
1 JOHN 4:18

I am Magnified by His mercy!
GENESIS 19:19

I am Magnifying the Lord of my life!
PSALM 40:16, 69:30

I am Marching forward in the things of God!
JOEL 2:7

I am Meditating on God's Word!
PSALM 1:1-2

I am Meek and shall delight myself in peace!
PSALM 37:11

I am Merciful!
2 SAMUEL 22:26, PSALM 18:25

I am Mindful of Christ in me!
COLOSSIANS 3:1, 2 PETER 3:2

I am Motivated by the Spirit of God!
LUKE 4:1

I am Mounting up with wings as an eagle!
ISAIAH 40:31

I am Moved by the Holy Spirit!
2 PETER 1:21

I am Moving forward with the Lord!
MARK 14:35

I am Moving up higher in Him!
PSALM 61:2

I am a Nation-changer!
1 PETER 2:9, GENESIS 21:18

I am a New Creation in Christ Jesus!
2 CORINTHIANS 5:17

I am filled with New Wine!
LUKE 5:38

I am Never forsaken!
HEBREWS 13:5

I am No longer denying the power of God!
2 TIMOTHY 3:5

I am No longer under condemnation!
ROMANS 8:1-2

I am Noble in Christ!
ESTHER 6:9

I am Nothing without Christ!
ROMANS 5:6

I am Nurtured by the Word of God!
PROVERBS 22:6

I am Nurturing!
EPHESIANS 6:4

I am an Oracle of God!
1 PETER 4:11

I am an Ornament of God's love and grace!
PROVERBS 1:9, 4:9, 1 PETER 3:4

I am an Overcomer by the blood of the lamb!
ROMANS 12:21, 1 JOHN 2:14, REVELATION 12:11

I am His Offspring!
ACTS 17:28

I am Obedient to His call!
DEUTERONOMY 4:30

I am Obedient to serve Him and shall spend
my days in prosperity!
JOB 36:11

I am Obeying the Spirit of God!
1 PETER 1:22

I am Oblated to the Lord!
PSALM 119:38

I am Observant of God's ways!
PROVERBS 23:26

I am Obtaining joy and gladness in my heart!
ISAIAH 35:10

I am Obtaining the Lord's favour!
PROVERBS 8:35

I am Occupying until He comes!
LUKE 19:13

I am of One mind!
1 PETER 3:8

I am One of a kind!
1 PETER 2:9

I am Offering praise to God continually!
HEBREWS 13:15

I am One with the Lord!
1 CORINTHIANS 6:17

I am Open-hearted!
PSALM 84:2

I am Openly receiving my reward!
MATTHEW 6:4

I am Operating in the gifts of the Spirit!
1 CORINTHIANS 14:12

I am Optimistic!
HEBREWS 13:6

I am Ordained by God!
JEREMIAH 1:5, JOHN 15:16

I am Osculated in the Lord's Presence!
2 CORINTHIANS 13:12

I am Outspoken for the Lord!
Acts 14:3, John 7:26

I am Outwardly living for Jesus!
Luke 20:38

I am Overflowing with God's goodness!
Leviticus 20:24

I am Overshadowed by His Son!
Matthew 17:5

I am Overwhelmed by God's love and goodness!
Psalm 61:2

I am a Pillar in the Kingdom!
GALATIANS 2:9

I am a Plumbline of spiritual truth!
AMOS 7:7-8

I am a Prayer warrior!
2 CHRONICLES 6:40, NEHEMIAH 1:6, PSALM 5:3

I am a Prayerful child of God!
1 THESSALONIANS 5:17

I am a vessel of Peace!
2 CORINTHIANS 13:11

I am a child of Peace because He loves me!
GALATIANS 5:22-23

I am at Peace with all people!
ROMANS 14:19

I am filled with Praise!
PSALM 139:14, 100:4

I am made Perfect in weakness!
2 CORINTHIANS 12:9

I am Partnered with the Holy One!
1 JOHN 4:4

I am Patient in the process of salvation!
2 SAMUEL 22:47, 1 CHRONICLES 16:23

I am Peculiar in God's kingdom!
EXODUS 19:5, DEUTERONOMY 14:2, TITUS 2:14

I am Perfect, of good comfort, of one mind,
and I live in peace!
1 PETER 3:8, PSALM 37:37

I am Perfected in the ways of God!
2 SAMUEL 22:31

I am Perfected in every good work to do His will!
HEBREWS 13:21

I am Perfectly created in God!
ROMANS 12:2

I am Permeated with His Presence!
ACTS 2:4

I am Persevering!
PHILIPPIANS 3:14

I am Persistent in God's call!
TITUS 3:8, LUKE 11:9-10

I am Personifying Christ's nature!
ACTS 17:28

I am Persuaded that nothing shall be able to
separate me from the love of God!
ROMANS 8:35

I am Planted in the house of the Lord and shall
flourish in the courts of my God!
PSALM 92:13

I am Planting seeds of honor!
PSALM 71:8

I am Pleasing the Lord in every thought,
word and deed!
1 JOHN 3:22

I am Plugged into Holy Ghost power!
PSALM 51:11, LUKE 11:13B

I am Pondering the Word of God!
PHILIPPIANS 4:8

I am Positioned in heavenly places!
EPHESIANS 2:6

I am Possessing my inheritance!
2 CORINTHIANS 6:10, ZECHARIAH 8:12

I am Possessing the land!
GENESIS 17:8, GENESIS 48:4, JOSHUA 1:6

I am Pouring out my heart before Him:
God is my refuge!
PSALM 46:1-3

I am Powerful by the Spirit of the Lord!
MICAH 3:8

I am Praising God for all things!
PSALM 34:1

I am Praising the Lord according to
His righteousness!
PSALM 34:1

I am Praying the will of God for my life!
PSALM 143:10

I am Praying with thanksgiving!
PHILIPPIANS 4:6

I am Praying without ceasing!
1 THESSALONIANS 5:17

I am Precious in the sight of God!
PSALM 116:15

I am Predestined to walk with God!
ROMANS 8:30, EPHESIANS 1:11, 2:10

I am Prepared for His banqueting house!
SONG OF SOLOMON 2:4

I am Presented faultless!
JUDE 1:24

I am Preserved by discretion and kept
by understanding!
DEUTERONOMY 6:24

I am Preserved by uprightness as I wait on Him!
PSALM 25:21

I am Preserved for a purpose!
2 TIMOTHY 4:18

I am Preserved for His heavenly kingdom!
JOHN 7:38

I am Preserved from trouble because the
Lord is my hiding place!
PSALM 32:7

I am Preserved in my going out and coming in,
even for evermore!
PSALM 121:8

I am Pressing toward the mark for the prize of
His high calling!
PHILIPPIANS 3:14

I am Privileged to be accepted in the Kingdom!
MATTHEW 25:34

I am Proclaiming liberty to the captives!
ISAIAH 61:1

I am Producing godly traits through believing
and pursuing His word!
1 TIMOTHY 4:7

I am Progressing in my relationship
with the Lord!
PSALM 73:25

I am Promoted by God!
PSALM 75:7, 75:6

I am Prospering according to God's Word!
PSALM 1:3, GENESIS 39:23

I am Prospering in health even as my
soul prospers!
3 JOHN 1:2

I am Prospering in the things of God!
GENESIS 39:3, JOSHUA 1:7

I am Protected with God's shield over me!
PSALM 27:5, JOHN 10:28

I am Proud to serve in God's kingdom!
ROMANS 12:11

I am Prudent!
PROVERBS 27:12

I am Pruned for Kingdom works!
JOHN 15:2

I am Purified as I hope in God!
1 JOHN 3:3

I am Purified by the Blood of Jesus!
TITUS 2:14

I am Purposefully following Christ!
EPHESIANS 1:9, ROMANS 8:28, ISAIAH 46:11

I am Pursuing total and complete healing!
JEREMIAH 33:3, 33:6

I am Quickened by the Word!
PSALM 119:50

I am Quickened by the Spirit that raised Jesus
from the dead!
1 PETER 2:9

I am Quickly confessing my sins to the Lord!
Psalm 32:5, DANIEL 9:20

I am a Quiet and gentle spirited child of God!
PSALM 37:11, ECCLESIASTES 4:6

I am a Representative of God's Kingdom!
COLOSSIANS 3:17

I am a Responsible child of God!
1 KINGS 3:12

I am a Royal Priesthood!
1 PETER 2:9

I am at Rest in God!
DEUTERONOMY 12:10

I am filled with Resurrection power!
ACTS 4:33, ROMANS 1:4

I am Radiant because He lives in me!
NUMBERS 6:25

I am Radiating God's love!
ROMANS 5:5

I am Raised up with Christ!
EPHESIANS 2:6, COLOSSIANS 2:12, ROMANS 6:4

I am Reading God's word daily!
DEUTERONOMY 17:19, EPHESIANS 3:4

I am Ready!
MATTHEW 24:44, LUKE 12:40

I am Reaping whatever I sow!
GALATIANS 6:8

I am Receiving all God has stored in
heaven for me!
JOB 22:22

I am Receiving the treasures of darkness and
hidden riches of secret places!
ISAIAH 45:3

I am Receiving my Father's good pleasure!
LUKE 12:32, EPHESIANS 1:5

I am Reconciled to my Heavenly Father!
ROMANS 5:10

I am Redeemed by the mighty hand of God!
PSALM 19:14, 27:1, 103:4

I am Redeemed from the curse of the law!
GALATIANS 3:13

I am Redeemed, I have been called by
His name; I am God's!
2 SAMUEL 4:9

I am Reflecting God's glory!
MATTHEW 16:27

I am Refusing to live in fear!
ISAIAH 43:1

I am Refusing to walk in agreement
with enemy lies!
JAMES 4:7

I am Refusing to be defeated by the enemy!
JAMES 4:7

I am Refusing to walk in agreement with lack!
DEUTERONOMY 2:7

I am Regaining my sight, spiritually and naturally!
MATTHEW 20:34

I am Rejoicing in God's plan for my life!
JEREMIAH 29:11, PSALM 68:3

I am Rejoicing in God's truth!
PSALM 19:8, 31:5

I am Rejoicing in the God of my salvation!
PSALM 33:21, 9:14

I am Rejoicing in the Lord!
PHILIPPIANS 4:4

I am Releasing all negativity unto the Lord!
MATTHEW 16:23

I am Releasing ungodly thoughts from my mind!
2 CORINTHIANS 10:5

I am Reliant upon the Lord!
2 CHRONICLES 13:18

I am Remaining steadfast in the Lord!
1 CORINTHIANS 15:58

I am Remembering Christ in communion!
1 CORINTHIANS 11:24-25

I am Rendering word curses and lies powerless!
JAMES 3:10

I am Renewed day by day!
PSALM 103:5, ROMANS 12:2, 2 CORINTHIANS 4:16

I am Renewed in the spirit of my mind!
EPHESIANS 4:22-24

I am Renewed like the eagle!
PSALM 103:5

I am Renewed with a right spirit!
PSALM 51:10

I am Renouncing ungodliness and worldly lusts!
TITUS 2:12

I am Repenting for not believing God's truths!
MARK 1:15

I am Representing the King of Kings!
REVELATION 17:14

I am Rescued by my Savior!
MATTHEW 18:11, JOHN 3:16

I am Resisting the devil as I submit myself to God!
JAMES 4:7

I am Resisting the devil with words of truth!
JAMES 4:7

I am Resonating with Holy Ghost power!
MATTHEW 22:29, MARK 12:24

I am Respected!
LEVITICUS 26:9

I am Resting because His presence goes with me!
PSALM 37:7

I am Resting in His loving arms!
ISAIAH 32:18

I am Resting in Hope!
PSALM 16:9

I am Retaining my integrity!
JOB 2:9, PROVERBS 4:4

I am Returning to my first love!
MARK 12:30, 1 JOHN 4:19

I am Reverencing the Lord!
LUKE 20:13

I am Rewarded...when I trust in the Lord God of Israel!
RUTH 2:12

I am Richly dwelling in godly wisdom!
COLOSSIANS 3:16

I am Righteous and holy!
EPHESIANS 4:24

I am Righteously serving the Lord!
GENESIS 15:6

I am Rightly dividing the word of truth!
2 TIMOTHY 2:15

I am Risen with Christ!
COLOSSIANS 3:1

I am Robed in righteousness!
ISAIAH 61:10

I am Rooted and grounded in love!
EPHESIANS 3:17

I am Rooted in righteousness, bearing good fruit!
PROVERBS 12:12

I am Ruling and Reigning with godly authority!
ISAIAH 32:1

I am Running the race set before me!
1 CORINTHIANS 9:24, HEBREWS 12:1

I am Running into His arms!
MARK 9:36, PSALM 91:4, DEUTERONOMY 33 :27

I am the Righteousness of God in Christ Jesus!
2 CORINTHIANS 5:21

I am a Saint who rejoices in goodness!
PSALM 16:3, 34:9, 2 CHRONICLES 6:41

I am a Scribe for the Lord!
MATTHEW 13:52, 1 CORINTHIANS 1:20

I am a Servant in the Kingdom of God!
MATTHEW 8:9, 24:45, ROMANS 1:1

I am a Servant of righteousness!
ROMANS 6:18

I am a Sheep of His pasture!
PSALM 23

I am a Shining Light!
MATTHEW 5:16

I am a Soldier in the army of the Lord!
2 TIMOTHY 2:3, 2:4

I am a Son of God through Christ Jesus!
GALATIANS 4:5

I am a Spirit-led child of God!
GALATIANS 5:18

I am a Student of the Word!
2 TIMOTHY 2:15

I am Safe in His arms!
PSALM 119:117

I am Sanctified!
ACTS 26:18, ROMANS 15:16

I am Satisfied with good things; my youth is
renewed like the eagle's!
PSALM 103:5, 2 PETER 1:5-7

I am Satisfied with His likeness!
PSALM 17:15

I am Saved and called with a holy calling!
ECCLESIASTES 3:1, 2 TIMOTHY 1:9

I am Saved by grace!
EPHESIANS 2:8, ROMANS 10:9, 5:15

I am Saved to the uttermost!
2 SAMUEL 22:4

I am Saved with an outstretched arm!
DEUTERONOMY 26:8

I am Sealed unto the day of redemption!
EPHESIANS 4:30

I am Sealed with that Holy Spirit of promise!
EPHESIANS 1:13

I am Seated in heavenly places!
EPHESIANS 1:3, 2:6

I am Secure in the name of Jesus!
PROVERBS 10:25

I am Seeking God's face!
PSALM 34:4

I am Seeking His will until I am found!
DEUTERONOMY 4:29

I am Seeking peace and pursuing it!
PSALM 34:14

I am Seeking the Father's heart to know Him,
that I am His child: and He is my God!
EXODUS 15:2, 2 PETER 1:17

I am Seeking the Kingdom of God and
His righteousness!
MATTHEW 6:33

I am Seeking the Lord while He may be found!
ISAIAH 55:6

I am Seeking the Lord and finding Him when I
search for Him with all my heart!
JEREMIAH 29:13

I am Serving a God who says nothing
is impossible!
LUKE 1:37

I am Serving a miracle-working God!
ACTS 2:22

I am Serving the Lord with joyfulness!
DEUTERONOMY 28:47

I am Set apart for holiness unto the Lord!
PSALM 4:3

I am Set upon a rock!
PSALM 27:5

I am Settled in my faith!
COLOSSIANS 1:23

I am Shielded with His armor!
EPHESIANS 6:14-17

I am Shining for the Lord!
MATTHEW 5:16

I am Significant in the living vine!
JOHN 15:5

I am Singing in my heart to the Lord!
JOHN 4:23-24, COLOSSIANS 3:16, EPHESIANS 5:19

I am Sitting at His feet!
LUKE 10:39, 10:42

I am Sitting at the right hand of the power of God!
LUKE 22:69

I am Sober and vigilant!
1 PETER 5:8

I am Sowing to the Spirit to reap
everlasting life!
GALATIANS 6:8

I am Speaking God's Word over
my circumstances!
ROMANS 4:17

I am Speaking words of life over myself
and others!
DEUTERONOMY 30:19

I am Speaking to myself in psalms, hymns
and spiritual songs, singing and making melody
in my heart to the Lord!
EPHESIANS 5:19

I am Spiritually minded!
ROMANS 8:6

I am Stable!
1 CHRONICLES 16:30

I am Standing in the liberty wherewith Christ
has made me free!
GALATIANS 5:1

I am Standing on the promises of God!
MALACHI 3:10, 2 CORINTHIANS 1:20

I am Standing on the Rock of my salvation!
2 SAMUEL 22:47

I am Standing perfect and complete in all
the will of God!
COLOSSIANS 4:12

I am Stilled in the presence of the Lord!
PSALM 46:10

I am Strengthened by the Lord!
DANIEL 10:19

I am Strengthened by trials!
2 CORINTHIANS 8:2

I am Stretched beyond measure!
2 CORINTHIANS 10:14

I am Striving for the faith of the gospel!
PHILIPPIANS 1:27

I am Strong and of a good courage...
for the Lord does go with me!
DEUTERONOMY 31:6

I am Strong in spirit and filled with wisdom!
LUKE 2:40

I am Strong in the Lord!
EXODUS 15:2, HABAKKUK 3:19

I am Studying to be quiet, doing my own
business and working with my hands!
1 THESSALONIANS 4:11

I am Subduing the earth!
GENESIS 1:28, PSALM 18:47

I am Submitted to the Lord!
1 PETER 2:12-14

I am Successful in all He has called me to do!
PSALM 8:6

I am Successful in God's eyes!
2 CHRONICLES 2:20B, JOSHUA 1:8

I am Sufficient in the Lord!
2 CORINTHIANS 12:9, 3:5

I am Surrounded with love!
PSALM 5:12

I am Sustained by the Lord!
PSALM 3:5

**I am Swift to hear, Slow to speak,
and Slow to wrath!**
JAMES 1:19

I am the Salt of the earth!
MATTHEW 5:13

I am the Seed of Abraham!
PSALM 105:6, GALATIANS 3:16

I am a Temperate child of God!
TITUS 1:8, 2:2

I am a Temple of the living God!
1 CORINTHIANS 3:16, 6:19, 2 CORINTHIANS 6:16

I am a Testimony of God's miracle-working power!
PSALM 136:4, EPHESIANS 3:7, PHILIPPIANS 2:13

I am a Three-part being!
1 THESSALONIANS 5:23

I am a Tree of life!
PROVERBS 11:30, MATTHEW 7:17

I am a Tree of righteousness!
ISAIAH 61:3

I am a vessel of Truth!
2 KINGS 20:3, PSALM 15:2, 25:5

I am come before His presence with Thanksgiving!
PSALM 69:30, 100:4

I am Taking heed that no man deceive me!
MATTHEW 24:4

I am Taking up the shield of faith!
EPHESIANS 6:16

I am Teachable in the ways of the Lord!
2 SAMUEL 22:35, JOB 32:7, 1 JOHN 2:27

I am Tenacious in the things of God!
PROVERBS 4:13

I am Tenderhearted, forgiving others like God!
EPHESIANS 4:32

I am Testifying of God's goodness!
2 CHRONICLES 6:41

I am Thankful for all things!
PSALM 100:4, EPHESIANS 5:20

I am Thankful unto the Lord for He is good!
1 CHRONICLES 16:34

I am Thinking on heavenly things!
JOHN 3:12

I am Thinking on good, pure and lovely things!
PHILIPPIANS 4:8

I am Thoughtful!
PSALM 48:9, 139:17, PROVERBS 16:3

I am Thriving in the Kingdom!
JOSHUA 1:8

I am Transformed by God's love and truth!
ROMANS 12:2

I am Transformed by the renewing of my mind!
ROMANS 12:2

I am Treasured in the Father's heart!
EXODUS 19:5

I am Tried by the Lord!
PSALM 11:5, 1 THESSALONIANS 2:4

I am Triumphant over my enemies!
1 CHRONICLES 17:10

I am Triumphant through the works of His hands!
PSALM 20:6

I am Trusting in God's infinite resources!
PHILIPPIANS 4:19

I am Trusting in God's mercy!
PSALM 52:8

I am Trusting in Him, my strength and shield!
PSALM 28:7

I am Trusting on the Lord to deliver me!
PSALM 22:8

I am Trustworthy!
PSALM 145:13

I am Truthful!
1 SAMUEL 12:24, 3 JOHN 1:4, JOHN 8:32

I am Turning to God with my whole heart!
ISAIAH 33:17, PSALM 80:3

I am Unalloyed for God!
PSALM 19:8, MATTHEW 5:8

I am Unanimously one with Christ!
2 CORINTHIANS 13:11

I am a vessel of God's Unconditional love!
JOHN 15:12

I am Undefiled!
HEBREWS 7:26

I am Understanding that wonderful peace of God!
PHILIPPIANS 4:7

I am Unequal with worldly ways!
1 CORINTHIANS 10:6

I am United as one spirit with the Lord!
1 CORINTHIANS 6:17

I am United in fellowship with like-minded believers!
PSALM 133:1

I am Unmovable in the work of the Lord!
1 CORINTHIANS 15:58

I am Unshakable!
LUKE 6:48, 2 THESSALONIANS 2:2

I am Upheld by His free spirit!
PSALM 51:12

I am Upheld by His righteous right hand!
PSALM 98:1, 37:24

I am Upright and shall dwell in His presence!
PSALM 140:13

I am Upright in heart!
PSALM 36:10, 18:23

I am a Vessel of love!
ROMANS 9:23

I am a Virtuous child of God!
RUTH 3:11

I am a Vital part of the body of Christ!
EPHESIANS 4:12

I am a Voice for the Lord!
ROMANS 15:19, PSALM 29:4

I am a vessel of Vitality!
PSALM 92:14, 1 PETER 1:3

I am inspired by God's Visions!
ACTS 2:17

I am living in Victory every day!
1 CORINTHIANS 15:57

I am of more Value than a sparrow!
MATTHEW 10:31

I am Valiant through Christ!
PSALM 60:12

I am Validated by God's Word!
1 CORINTHIANS 1:6, HEBREWS 6:17

I am Valiant through God; He treads
down my enemies!
2 SAMUEL 2:7

I am Victorious by His right hand and
His holy arm!
PSALM 98:1

I am Victorious in Christ!
1 CHRONICLES 29:11, 1 CORINTHIANS 15:57

I am Vigilant!
1 PETER 5:8

I am a vessel of Worship!
1 Samuel 15:25

I am a Watchman!
Ezekiel 3:17

I am a Well of living water!
John 4:10, 7:38

I am a Winner in Christ Jesus!
Philippians 3:8

I am a Witness for Christ!
Acts 1:8

I am a Workman worthy of my hire!
Luke 10:7

I am a Writer called to inspire others!
Psalm 144:1

I am filled with God's Wisdom!
Exodus 31:3, Luke 2:40

I am Waiting on the Lord with good courage,
and he shall strengthen my heart!
Psalm 27:14, 31:24

I am Waiting upon God: from His Son
cometh my salvation!
1 CORINTHIANS 1:7

I am Walking in agreement with God's
plan for my life!
JOHN 20:31

I am Walking in divine health!
3 JOHN 1:2

I am Walking in freedom!
ACTS 22:28

I am Walking in grace and glory: no good thing
will be withheld from me for walking uprightly!
PSALM 84:11

I am Walking in love!
EPHESIANS 5:2

I am Walking in newness of life!
ROMANS 6:4

I am Walking in Obedience!
DEUTERONOMY 30:20

I am Walking in the light!
1 JOHN 1:7

I am Walking in the Spirit!
ROMANS 8:2, 8:4, GALATIANS 5:16, 5:25

I am Walking in truth!
1 JOHN 3:3

I am Washed, sanctified and justified!
1 CORINTHIANS 6:11

I am Washed with the precious Blood of Jesus!
1 CORINTHIANS 6:11, REVELATION 1:5

I am Washed from iniquities and cleansed
from all sin!
PSALM 51:2

I am Watering godly seed planted in my life!
MATTHEW 13:23

I am Weakening the enemy by speaking
God's truths!
JOHN 10:10

I am Wealthy for the Kingdom!
DEUTERONOMY 8:18, 1 SAMUEL 2:7

I am Wearing godly armor!
EPHESIANS 6:11

I am Whole and complete in Christ!
MATTHEW 9:21, 14:36, COLOSSIANS 4:12

I am Willing and obedient...I shall eat the
good of the land!
ISAIAH 1:19

I am Willing to be God's clay!
JEREMIAH 18:6, ISAIAH 64:8

I am Wise as a serpent and harmless as a dove!
MATTHEW 10:16

I am Wise to hear and increase learning!
PROVERBS 1:5, 16:23

I am Wise to observe godly ways!
PSALM 19:7

I am Working out my own salvation with
fear and trembling!
PHILIPPIANS 2:12

I am Worshipful!
PSALM 5:7

I am Worshiping the Lord in the beauty of
His holiness!
PSALM 96:9

I am Worth redeeming!
EXODUS 15:13, PSALM 26:11

I am Worthy of God's love!
2 SAMUEL 22:4, EPHESIANS 4:1, COLOSSIANS 1:10

I am Worthy to take up my cross and
follow Christ!
MATTHEW 10:37-38

I am Wrapped in my Savior's embrace!
SONG OF SOLOMON 2:6

I am a Yielded vessel of God!
2 CHRONICLES 30:8

I am Yielded unto God!
ROMANS 6:13

I am Yielding good fruit!
MATTHEW 7:17, EZEKIEL 17:8

I am Yoked with Christ!
MATTHEW 11:29

I am Youthful!
ECCLESIASTES 11:9, PSALM 103:5

I am filled with Zeal!
TITUS 2:14

I am Zealous for the Lord!
1 CORINTHIANS 14:12

About the Writer

Kathleen Schubitz was born in Chicago and lived in the Midwestern United States most of her life. She served more than ten years at the headquarters of Rotary International, and worked much of the time as production assistant for *The Rotarian* Magazine. She relocated to Florida in 1990.

In spite of an oppressive childhood, Kathleen pressed through abuse and sickness as an adult, turning tragedy into triumph and life's hardships into stepping stones for success.

In 2004, the Lord gave Kathleen the company name, and in faith and obedience, RPJ & Company, Inc. (Romans 14:17) was established. As owner and founder, she set out to bless pastors, leaders, ministers, missionaries and others by offering to publish work to enhance the Body of Christ. As a designer, poet, author and speaker, she brings unique experience to the task of publishing.

Editing, proofreading and eye for detail are just a few outstanding traits she brings to her work as a publisher. She has blossomed in her workmanship, which is demonstrated in books, calendars, business cards, bookmarks, brochures and particularly in the poetry book genre.

"I count it an honor and privilege to work with so many talented authors and artists throughout the world. What a blessing to offer them more than their published book, rather a special creation designed with each author in mind," she stated recently.

Learn more about publishing your work with Kathleen Schubitz by visiting www.rpjandco.com.